Organ Hymns of Faith

Harmonizations of Hymns
for Congregational Singing
arranged by
Mark Thallander

Table of Contents

© 2004 by Fred Bock Music Company. All rights reserved. Made in U.S.A.

Fred Bock Music Company

Foreword

I have great admiration and respect for the abilities of Mark Thallander. He was my long time associate at the Crystal Cathedral, where he excelled in both administration and in service playing. His approach to the latter was always fitting and often quite stirring.

In this new collection of hymn arrangements he brings his hallmark sense of beauty and excitement coupled with his unique harmonic language and colorful expression linked to each hymn text.

Mark is not only gifted, he has incredible spirit . When this book is issued to coincide with a service and concert in his honor on March 21, 2004, it will remind us that less than eight months before Mark lost his left arm in a horrific car accident. His strong faith, super-positive outlook on life and amazing resourcefulness have him up, active, and making an incredible new life for himself. He is playing the organ again, and composed two of the arrangements in this collection to go with those written earlier.

I treasure Mark's friendship of many years, and find enormous inspiration in what he has done and in what he is accomplishing despite physical challenges that would overwhelm most people.

As you and your listeners enjoy playing and hearing the arrangements, give thanks that God not only spared Mark's life, but obviously still has great plans for him as he serves Him in ministering to others.

Frederick Swann
National President, American Guild of Organist,
Organist Emeritus, The Crystal Cathedral,
Organist Emeritus, First Congregational Church of Los Angeles

Introduction

"Take my hands and let them move at the impulse of Thy love;
take my feet and let them be swift and beautiful for Thee."

The words of this hymn had become my weekly prayer before starting the organ prelude. However, on January 25, 2004, my first time to play a complete Sunday morning service since my accident of August 3, 2003, I prayed differently. *"Take my hand…"*. I then asked Jesus to be present – to be my strength in weakness - that the organ music would sound complete – and that in some awesome spiritual sense, He would be my left hand.

I began with Fred Bock's majestic setting of *Old Hundredth*. And then that "historic" service at Bel Air Presbyterian Church continued. John West, artist-in-residence, had carefully crafted the worship to ensure my success. The choir was praying for me.

During the greeting time, a woman said to me, "I had no idea your arm had been amputated until the pastor mentioned it in the middle of the service." My prayer had been answered. Jesus had come along side me. I was not alone in that service. And you are not alone, either. He will never leave us or forsake us!

May these arrangements serve to assist you and your congregation in offering praise and worship to our loving and faithful God!

Mark Thallander

P.S. We have provided suggested metronome markings knowing that the acoustics of your worship space may require some variation. Where suggested dynamic markings and/or crescendo passages are indicated, you may wish to couple the enclosed divisions with principal chorus, mixture(s) and reed chorus, and use the swell boxes to accomplish the desired result. Registration for first and last stanzas should generally be full organ; middle stanzas may be based on textual consideration and variety of sounds. Enjoy!

Praise the Lord! O Heavens, Adore Him

AUSTRIAN HYMN
Franz Joseph Haydn
Arranged by Mark Thallander

© Copyright 2004 by Fred Bock Music Company.
All rights reserved.   Made in U.S.A.
www.FredBockMusicCompany.com

Interlude

trumpets

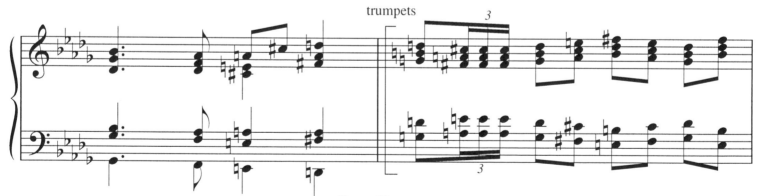

Broadly

Final stanza

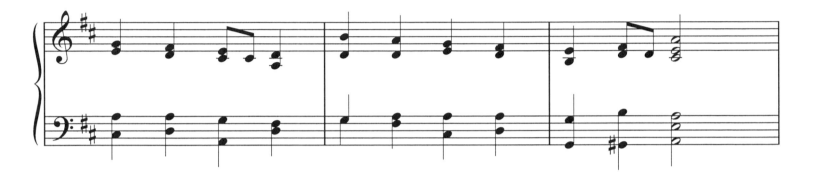

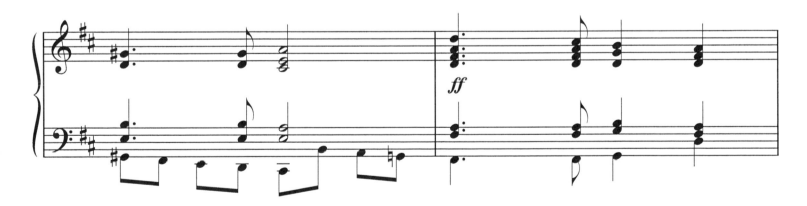

O Worship the King

LYONS
Johann Michael Haydn
Arranged by Mark Thallander

Majestically ♩ = 112

© Copyright 2004 by Fred Bock Music Company.
All rights reserved.   Made in U.S.A.
www.FredBockMusicCompany.com

Interlude

trumpets

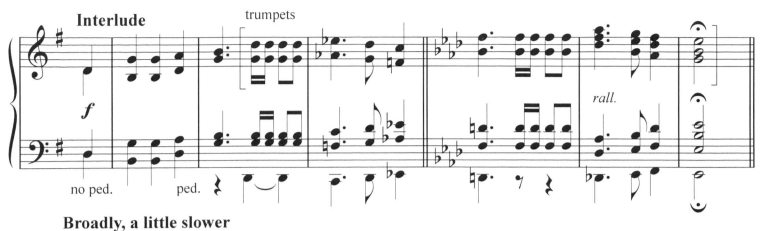

Broadly, a little slower
Final stanza

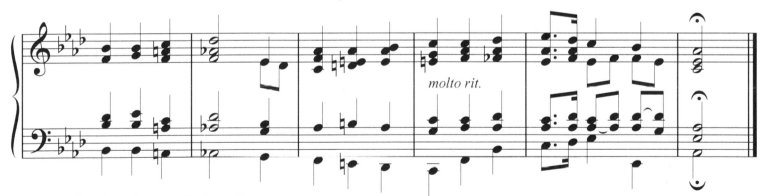

Optional extended ending

trumpets

*If used, omit the last measure and molto ritard in the system above.

Sing Praise to God Who Reigns Above

MIT FREUDEN ZART
Bohemian Brethren's *Kirchengesänge*, 1566
Arranged by Mark Thallander

Joyfully ♩ = 80

Introduction

Stanza(s)

© Copyright 2004 by Fred Bock Music Company.
All rights reserved.   Made in U.S.A.
www.FredBockMusicCompany.com

Interlude

Final stanza

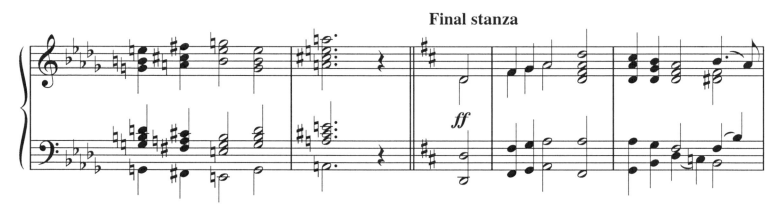

O the Deep, Deep Love of Jesus

EBENEZER (TON-Y-BOTEL)
Thomas J. Williams
Arranged by Mark Thallander

Stately ♩ = 72

Introduction

Stanza(s)

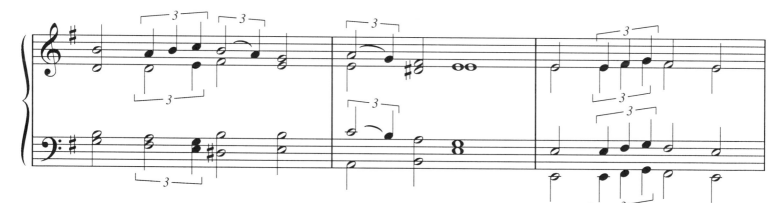

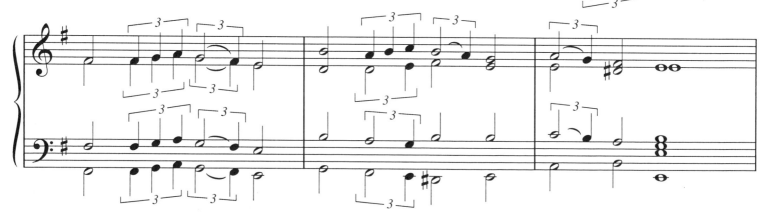

© Copyright 2004 by Fred Bock Music Company.
All rights reserved.   Made in U.S.A.
www.FredBockMusicCompany.com

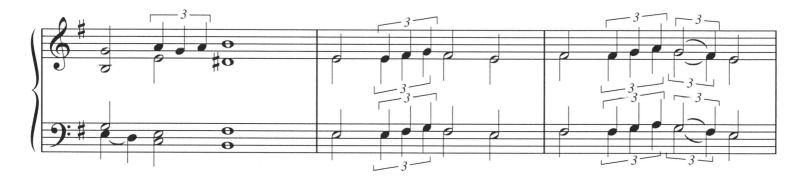

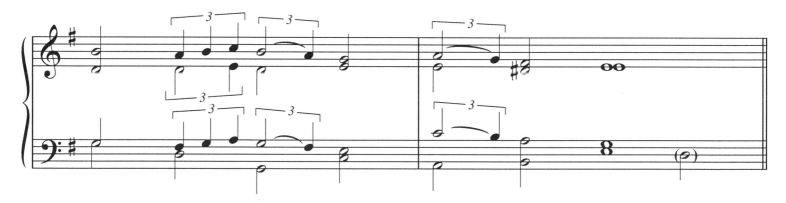

Interlude

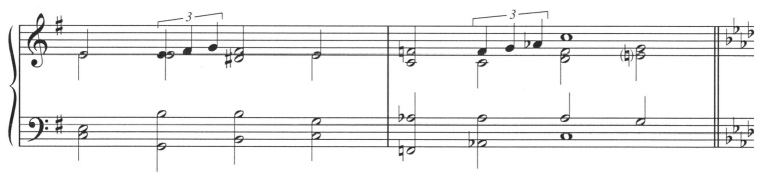

Final stanza

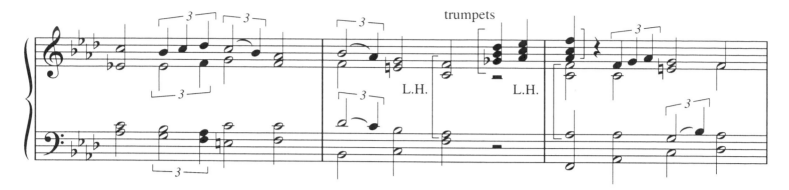

trumpets

L.H.   L.H.

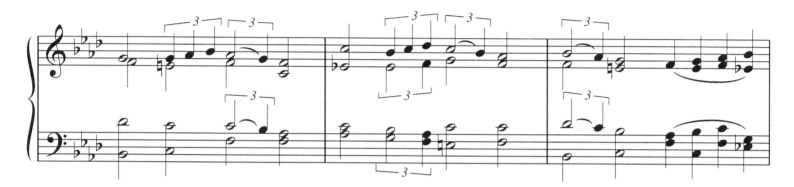

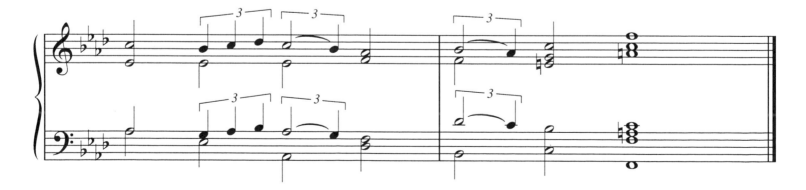

Our Great Savior

HYFRYDOL
Rowland H. Prichard
Arranged by Mark Thallander

Jubilant ♩ = 120

Introduction

Stanza(s)
a tempo

© Copyright 2004 by Fred Bock Music Company.
All rights reserved.   Made in U.S.A.
www.FredBockMusicCompany.com

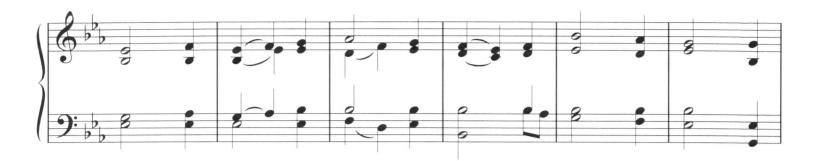

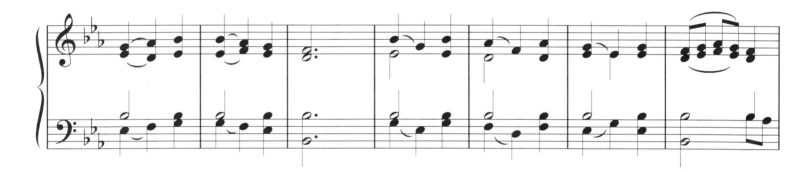

Interlude

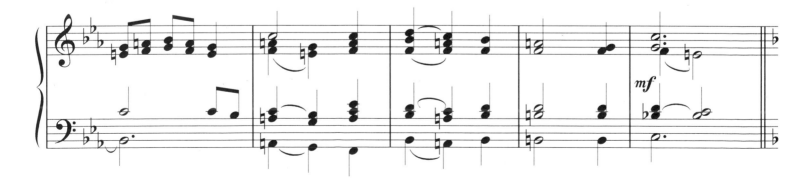

Stanza(s)

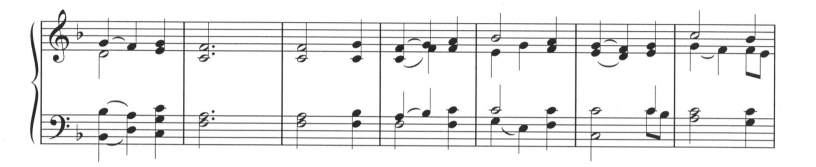

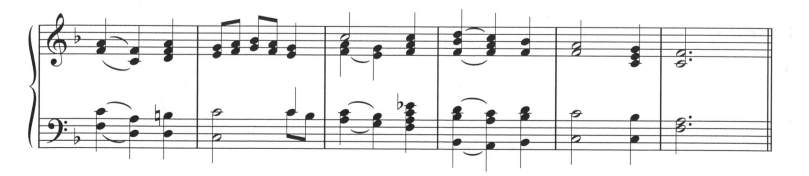

Interlude

Final Stanza

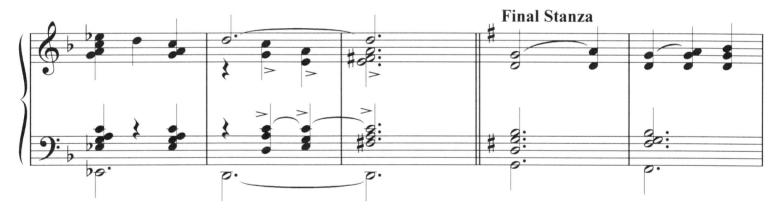

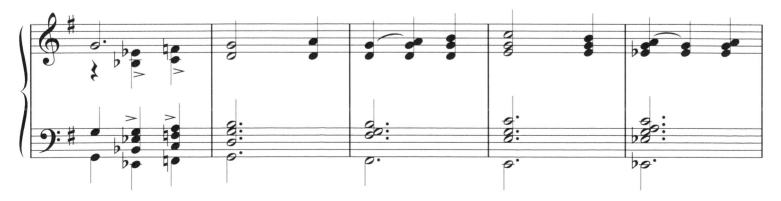

Fervently

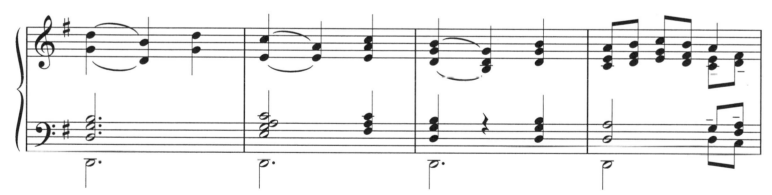

Broadly

molto rit.

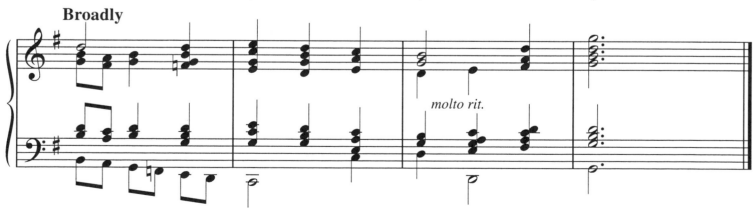

We Praise You, O God, Our Redeemer

KREMSER
Netherlands Folk Song
Arranged by Mark Thallander

Spirited ♩ = 108

Introduction

Stanza(s)

© Copyright 2004 by Fred Bock Music Company.
All rights reserved.   Made in U.S.A.
www.FredBockMusicCompany.com

Interlude
trumpets

Final stanza

Angels from the Realms of Glory

REGENT SQUARE
Henry T. Smart
Arranged by Mark Thallander

Joyfully ♩ = 100

Introduction

Stanza(s)

© Copyright 2004 by Fred Bock Music Company.
All rights reserved.   Made in U.S.A.
www.FredBockMusicCompany.com

Interlude

poco a poco rit.

Broadly
Final stanza

ff

molto rit.

+32'

Jesus Shall Reign

DUKE STREET
John Hatton
Arranged by Mark Thallander

Triumphantly ♩ = 60

Introduction

Stanza(s)

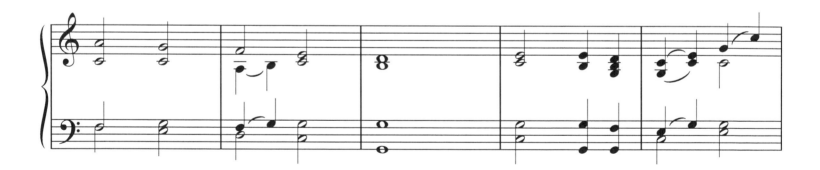

© Copyright 2004 by Fred Bock Music Company.
All rights reserved.   Made in U.S.A.
www.FredBockMusicCompany.com

23

Interlude

Stanza(s)

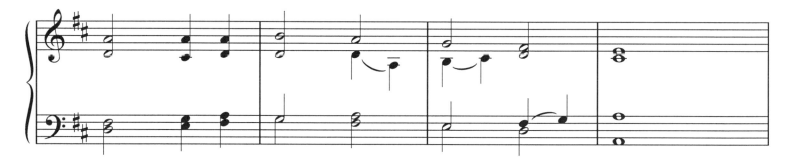

Interlude

Final Stanza

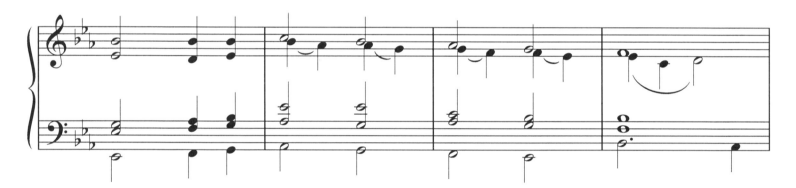

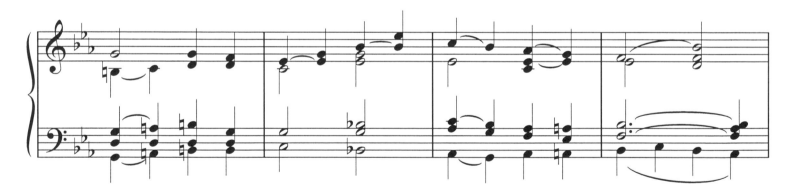

molto rit.